Sanjeev Kapoor's
KHAZANA

Mirch Mazaa

In association with Alyona Kapoor

Popular Prakashan
www.popularprakashan.com

Published by
POPULAR PRAKASHAN PVT. LTD.
301, Mahalaxmi Chambers
22, Bhulabhai Desai Road
Mumbai - 400026
for KHANA KHAZANA PUBLICATIONS PVT. LTD.

First Published 2009

(4321)
ISBN: 978-81-7991-573-8

Design: Namita Jadhav

PRINTED IN INDIA
by Sanat Printers
Plot No. 312, EPIP Kundli 131028
Sonepat Haryana.

Author's note

Chile, capsicum, paprika, pimento, red pepper, aji, cayenne pepper, piri-piri... a chilli by any other name will be just as fiery! Or not – there are some chillies that produce a mild tingling of the tongue and most others that set your mouth on fire!

Who would have thought that this fruit (yes, fruit!) that is an essential ingredient in Indian cooking was virtually unknown to our subcontinent till the Portuguese explorer Vasco Da Gama landed at Goa in the 15th century. Since then, chillies have been rapidly absorbed into Indian cuisine, which today appears bland and characterless without their sharp bite. So indispensable are they to the Indian palate, that today India is the largest producer of chillies!

From their first South American origins, chillies have evolved and multiplied to over 400 varieties all over the world. In India some of the most common are *Bedgi, Kashmiri, Sankeshwari, Guntur, Naga Jolokia, Dhani, Hindpur, Ellachipur Sannam, Kanthari-White, Madras Pari, Tomato Chilli (Warangal Chappatta).* Of these the *Naga Jolokia* that grows in Tezpur, Assam, has the distinction of being the world's hottest chilli.

This potent fruit, a member of the capsicum family, starts out green and then turns flaming red when it ripens. Dried at that stage it can be used whole to season a dish, ground with spices to form a rich red paste or crushed to a fine powder.

When green, chillies add a delicate, fresh heat and crunch to curries and kababs.

Mirch Mazaa celebrates the chilli and the sheer enjoyment it provides to our taste buds! I have put together a collection of recipes based on this hot favourite, which I have chosen from cuisines across the world. Try out the delicious Goan Chilli Chicken, crisp Mozzarella-stuffed Chillies, wholesome Chilli-Garlic Noodles, yummy Chilli-Garlic Okra, delectable Mirchi ka Salan or luscious Mirchi Murgh and you will be coming back for more!

All the recipes are meant for four portions when they form a part of a menu that has other complementary dishes. As you will see, all the recipes are written in a simple step-by-step manner which you will find very easy to follow.

So turn the heat up and serve yourself a generous portion of *mazaa* that only a *mirch* can generate!

Happy cooking!

Contents

Soups & Salads

Snacks

Main Course

HOT AND SOUR CHICKEN SOUP

Ingredients

¼ cup boneless chicken, boiled and chopped

1 slice bamboo shoot

3 tablespoons cornflour

2 tablespoons oil

1 small onion, chopped

2-3 garlic cloves, chopped

1 inch ginger, grated

2 inches celery stalk, chopped

½ medium carrot, grated

1 tablespoon chopped cabbage

2 fresh button mushrooms, chopped

½ medium green capsicum, chopped

2 french beans, chopped

½ teaspoon white pepper powder

Salt to taste

½ teaspoon sugar

½ teaspoon MSG (optional)

2 tablespoons soy sauce

2 tablespoons green chilli sauce

4-5 cups Chicken Stock (page 79)

2 tablespoons white vinegar

1 tablespoon Chilli Oil (page 94)

1 spring onion green stalk, chopped

METHOD

1. Boil the bamboo shoot in one cup of water for two to three minutes; drain, cool and chop.
2. Mix the cornflour in half a cup of water.
3. Heat the oil in a wok or saucepan; add the onion, garlic and ginger and stir-fry for a few seconds.
4. Add the bamboo shoot, celery, carrot, cabbage, mushrooms, capsicum and French beans; sauté for two to three minutes or until the vegetables are almost cooked, stirring continuously. Add the chicken and sauté for one minute.
5. Add the white pepper powder, salt to taste, sugar, MSG, soy sauce and green chilli sauce; mix well.
6. Stir in the chicken stock and bring to a boil. Stir in the cornflour mixture and continue to cook for one minute, or until the soup thickens, stirring continuously.
7. Stir in the vinegar, drizzle the chilli oil over the soup and serve piping hot, garnished with spring onion green.

CHEF'S TIP

We have used tinned bamboo shoot slices, which are preserved in brine, hence they have to be boiled in water before use.

MUSHROOM SOUP WITH CHILLIES

INGREDIENTS

20-25 fresh button mushrooms, quartered

4 cups Vegetable Stock (*see below*)

1 tablespoon oil

Salt to taste

1 inch ginger, cut into strips

¼ cup chopped fresh coriander

4-5 spring onion green stalks, chopped

Chilli Paste

1 tablespoon oil

4 dried red chillies, halved

4 shallots, chopped

3 garlic cloves, chopped

1 inch galangal, sliced

METHOD

1. For the chilli paste, heat the oil in a pan; add the dried red chillies, shallots, garlic and galangal and sauté for four to five minutes. Cool and grind to a fine paste.
2. For the soup, heat one tablespoon of oil in a separate pan; add the mushrooms

and sauté for one minute. Transfer the mushrooms to a plate.

3. To the same pan, add the vegetable stock and bring to a boil.
4. Add the salt, sautéed mushrooms and ginger strips.
5. Stir in the chilli paste and simmer for five minutes.
6. Sprinkle fresh coriander and spring onion greens over the soup and serve hot.

VEGETABLE STOCK

Place 1 sliced onion, 1 sliced carrot, a 2-3 inch piece of celery, 2 garlic cloves, 1 bay leaf, 5-6 black peppercorns and 2-3 cloves in a pan with 5 cups of water and bring to a boil. Simmer for 15 minutes and strain.

SPICY PINEAPPLE BOAT

INGREDIENTS

2-3 green chillies

1 medium pineapple

2 medium apples

1 small papaya

2 medium pears

½ medium pomegranate

2 medium oranges

1 tablespoon lemon juice

Black salt to taste

3 tablespoons orange juice

METHOD

1. Halve the pineapple lengthways. Scoop the flesh out without damaging the shell and cut the flesh into half-inch cubes.
2. Wash, core and cut the apples into half-inch cubes.
3. Peel, halve, deseed and cut the papaya into half-inch cubes. Wash the green chillies and grind to a coarse paste.
4. Wash and cut the pears into half-inch cubes. Separate the pomegranate kernels from the pomegranate.
5. Peel the orange, remove segments, discard the seeds and cut each orange segment into three pieces.
6. Mix all the fruits with lemon juice, green chilli paste, black salt and orange juice. Serve this in the halved pineapple boats.

ALOO MIRCH KA SALAD

INGREDIENTS

16-18 baby potatoes

2 teaspoons red chilli flakes

2-3 green chillies, seeded and chopped

1 tablespoon oil

2 tablespoons lemon juice

1 teaspoon sugar

Salt to taste

10-12 black peppercorns, crushed

1 tablespoon tomato ketchup

A few sprigs of fresh coriander, chopped

METHOD

1 Preheat an oven to 180°C/350°F/Gas Mark 4. Scrub and wash the baby potatoes well, prick with a fork and rub the oil over the surface. Roast the potatoes in the preheated oven for thirty to forty minutes or till tender.

2. Cut the potatoes in half, leaving the skins on.

3. Combine the lemon juice, sugar, salt, chilli flakes, green chillies, peppercorns and tomato ketchup in a large bowl. Add the potatoes and toss well to mix. Serve, garnished with chopped fresh coriander.

CHILLI-CHEESE CHAKRI

Ingredients

3-4 green chillies, slit and seeded

200 grams cream cheese, mashed to a paste

4 tortillas

2 fresh red chillies, chopped

½ teaspoon crushed red chillies

Salt to taste

2 tablespoons tomato ketchup

1 medium onion, peeled and chopped

2 tablespoons fresh coriander, chopped

A few fresh mint leaves

Method

1. Chop the chillies very finely. Add to the cream cheese. Add the chopped fresh red chillies and crushed red chillies; mix well. Add salt to taste and the tomato ketchup. Mix well.
2. Add the onion and fresh coriander and mix once again.
3. Heat a pan and warm the tortillas on both sides to soften.
4. Spread the warmed tortillas on a flat surface and spread a portion of the chilli-cheese mixture over the tortilla.
5. Roll the tortillas up tightly. Place them in the refrigerator for fifteen minutes.
6. Cut diagonally into small round slices and serve garnished with fresh mint leaves.

SICHUAN CHILLI POTATOES

INGREDIENTS

1 tablespoon vinegar

8-10 Sichuan peppers, crushed (optional)

4-5 whole dried red chillies, broken into bites

1 teaspoon red chilli paste

4-5 medium potatoes

3 tablespoons cornflour

2 tablespoons oil + for deep-frying

1 medium onion, sliced

5-6 garlic cloves, finely chopped

1 teaspoon soy sauce

½ teaspoon sugar

Salt to taste

1 spring onion green stalk, roughly chopped

METHOD

1. Peel and cut each potato into ten to twelve thick wedges. Soak in cold water for half an hour. Heat sufficient water and parboil the potato wedges. Drain and cool.
2. Dust the parboiled potatoes with one and a half tablespoons of cornflour.

3. Mix the remaining cornflour in a quarter cup of water. Heat sufficient oil in a wok and deep-fry for two minutes or until golden brown and completely cooked and crisp. Drain on absorbent paper.
4. Heat two tablespoons of oil in a wok, add the broken red chillies and stir-fry for half a minute. Immediately add the Sichuan peppers, onion and garlic and continue to stir-fry.
5. Stir in the red chilli paste mixed with two tablespoons of water, soy sauce, sugar and salt. Stir-fry for half a minute.
6. Add the fried potatoes and toss to heat through.
7. Stir in the cornflour mixture, toss well to mix and add the vinegar. Stir-fry for half a minute and serve garnished with spring onion green.

CHILLI PANEER

INGREDIENTS

3-4 green chillies, sliced

200 grams cottage cheese

2 tablespoons oil + for deep-frying

4 tablespoons cornflour

3-4 garlic cloves, crushed

2 medium onions, cut into thick slices

1 large green capsicum, seeded and cut into thick strips

½ cup Vegetable Stock (page 12)

Salt to taste

½ teaspoon white pepper powder

2 tablespoons soy sauce

¼ teaspoon MSG (optional)

METHOD

1. Drain the cottage cheese well and cut into medium-sized cubes. Heat sufficient oil in a wok. Roll the cottage cheese in cornflour and deep-fry on medium heat till the edges start to turn brown. Remove, drain on absorbent paper and set aside.
2. Mix the remaining cornflour in a little water and set aside.

3. Heat two tablespoons oil in a wok, add the crushed garlic and stir-fry for a minute. Add the green chillies, onions and capsicum. Sauté for a couple of minutes or until almost cooked.
4. Add the fried cottage cheese and stir in the vegetable stock. Add the salt, white pepper powder, soy sauce and MSG, and stir well.
5. Add the cornflour mixture and cook on high heat until the sauce thickens and coats the cottage cheese and the vegetables. Serve hot immediately.

CRISPY SPRING ROLLS WITH SWEET CHILLI DIP

INGREDIENTS

¼ cup rice vermicelli

2 spring onions, finely chopped

1 egg

3 tablespoons oil

1 inch ginger, chopped

1 medium carrot, grated

¼ cup bean sprouts

8-10 spinach leaves, chopped

A few sprigs of fresh coriander, chopped

2 tablespoons soy sauce

Salt to taste

¼ teaspoon white pepper powder

¼ teaspoon MSG (optional)

10-12 Spring Roll Wrappers (*see below*)

Oil for deep-frying

Sweet Chilli Dip

¼ cup sugar

½ cup rice vinegar

2 fresh red chillies

Salt to taste

METHOD

1. For the sweet chilli dip, place the sugar in a small pan with one-fourth cup of water. Heat gently, stirring continuously till the sugar dissolves. Boil it gently till it forms a light syrup. Stir in the red chillies, salt and rice vinegar and leave to cool completely.
2. Break the egg, mix lightly and set aside. Boil the vermicelli in sufficient water with one tablespoon of oil till almost cooked, drain, refresh in cold water and keep aside.
3. Heat the remaining oil in a wok, add chopped ginger and stir-fry for fifteen seconds. Add the onion and grated carrots and stir-fry for few minutes.
4. Add the bean sprouts, chopped spinach, fresh coriander, soy sauce and boiled vermicelli and stir for another minute. Add salt, white pepper and MSG and mix. Set aside to cool.
5. Place a spring roll wrapper on the work surface. Place two tablespoonful of the filling in the centre. Fold over the wrapper to encase the filling completely.
6. Fold in each side, then roll up tightly. Brush the end with the egg to seal (you can use a paste of refined flour and water to replace egg). Repeat until all the filling has been used.
7. Heat sufficient oil and deep-fry the spring rolls in batches until golden and crisp. Drain on absorbent paper. Serve hot with the sweet chilli dip.

Spring Roll Wrappers

Ingredients

¼ cup refined flour

1 cup + 1 tablespoon cornflour

Salt to taste

Oil for greasing

Method

1. To make spring roll wrappers, mix one cup of cornflour, the refined flour and salt to taste in a mixing bowl.
2. Add two cups of water and whisk thoroughly. Strain the batter and set aside for fifteen minutes. Adjust the consistency of the batter by adding a little water if required.
3. Heat an eight-inch non-stick frying pan; brush with a little oil and pour a ladleful of batter into it. Swirl to coat the bottom of the pan and pour the excess batter back into the bowl.
4. Cook over moderate heat till the edges start curling. Peel off or remove in one swift motion. Cool and sprinkle with a little cornflour. Repeat the process to make ten to twelve wrappers.

CHILLI CHICKEN

INGREDIENTS

6-8 green chillies, sliced

2 tablespoons chilli sauce

400 grams boneless chicken

2 eggs

2½ tablespoons cornflour

Salt to taste

2 tablespoons soy sauce

1 tablespoon oil + for deep-frying

8-10 garlic cloves, peeled and chopped

2 medium onions, peeled and cut into thick slices

2 medium green capsicums, seeded and cut into thick strips

¼ teaspoon MSG (optional)

½ teaspoon black peppercorns, crushed

2 tablespoons vinegar

METHOD

1. Wash, trim and cut the chicken into fingers. Mix together the eggs, two tablespoons cornflour, salt, and one tablespoon each of soy sauce and chilli sauce in a bowl. Marinate the chicken in this mixture for half an hour.

2. Mix the remaining cornflour with three tablespoons of water.
3. Heat sufficient oil in a wok and deep-fry the marinated chicken till crisp. Remove and drain on absorbent paper.
4. Heat one tablespoon of oil in a wok or a pan, add the chopped garlic and stir-fry for a few seconds. Add the onions and green chillies. Continue to stir-fry for a couple of minutes.
5. Add the capsicum strips and sauté for a few seconds. Add the remaining soy sauce and chilli sauce, MSG, salt, crushed peppercorns and cornflour mixture. Stir in the vinegar.
6. Add the fried chicken and sauté till the sauce coats the chicken.
7. Serve hot.

CHILLI TACOS

INGREDIENTS

2 green chillies, chopped

2 teaspoons chilli sauce

8 taco shells

A few sprigs of fresh mint

1 cup baked beans in tomato sauce

½ cup low-fat cheese, grated

2 spring onions, chopped

2 tablespoons lemon juice

Salt to taste

½ teaspoon black pepper powder

½ bunch lettuce (preferably iceberg), shredded

½ cup Cheddar cheese, grated

8 cherry tomatoes, quartered

METHOD

1. Chop half the fresh mint reserving some for garnishing.
2. Warm the taco shells in a preheated oven for a few minutes.
3. In a bowl, mix together the baked beans, grated cheese, spring onions, chillies, chilli sauce, lemon juice and chopped mint. Add the salt and pepper powder, mix lightly.

4. Fill the taco shells till about three-fourth full with shredded lettuce and spoon the baked bean mixture on top of the shredded lettuce leaves evenly.
5. Top the shells with the grated Cheddar cheese, quartered cherry tomatoes and a sprig of mint.
6. Serve immediately.

Chef's Tip

Though the taco shells are fried, since the quantity of salad used is more it becomes a healthy meal with controlled calories.

PIQUANT CHICKEN WINGS

Ingredients

16 chicken wings

1 cup orange juice

Salt to taste

2 tablespoons cornflour

1 teaspoon black peppercorns, crushed

2 teaspoons crushed red chillies

3 tablespoons honey

2 tablespoons lemon juice

Method

1. Trim and wash the chicken wings and shape into lollipops. Place in a bowl and add orange juice and salt. Marinate for ten to fifteen minutes.
2. Mix the cornflour and half a cup of water.
3. Take the lollipops out of the marinade, and cook the marinade till it reduces a little and thickens.
4. Add the lollipops, half the crushed peppercorns, crushed red chillies and honey. Cook over high heat for five to ten minutes.
5. When the chicken is nearly done, stir in the cornflour mixture. Cook for one minute and add the lemon juice.
6. Sprinkle with the remaining crushed peppercorns and serve.

MOZZARELLA-STUFFED CHILLIES

INGREDIENTS

8 Bhavnagri chillies, slit and seeded

8 pickled jalapeño chillies, slit and seeded

1 cup grated mozzarella cheese

2 teaspoons dried mixed herbs

1 cup cornflour

Salt to taste

2 cups fresh breadcrumbs

Oil for deep-frying

METHOD

1. Mix the grated cheese and dried mixed herbs in a bowl. Stuff the mixture into the chillies.
2. Mix the cornflour, salt and two-third cup of water to make a batter.
3. Dip the chillies in the batter and roll them in the breadcrumbs. Repeat the process to get a double coating.
4. Heat the oil in a deep pan till very hot and deep-fry the chillies till golden brown.
5. Drain on absorbent paper. Serve hot.

HOT CHILLI CORN

Ingredients

2 cups corn kernels, boiled

1 teaspoon red chilli flakes

1 green chilli, chopped

1 tablespoon lemon juice

1 small green capsicum, seeded and chopped

1 small red capsicum, seeded and chopped

Salt to taste

¼ teaspoon peppercorns, crushed

2 tablespoons fresh coriander, chopped

Method

1. Heat a non-stick pan. Add the boiled corn kernels, red chilli flakes and green chilli and cook for a minute.
2. Add the lemon juice, green and red capsicums, and salt. Cover the pan and allow them to soften for about two minutes.
3. Mix well. Add the crushed peppercorns and serve garnished with the fresh coriander.

CHILLI FISH CAKES

Ingredients

500 grams boneless fish fillets (such as *ghol*)

Salt to taste

1 tablespoon lemon juice

2 tablespoons oil + for shallow-frying

1 inch ginger, chopped

12 garlic cloves, chopped

1 medium onion, chopped

1 six-inch celery stalk, chopped

2 teaspoons red chilli paste

2 tablespoons white vinegar

½ cup cornflour

¼ teaspoon white pepper powder

2 tablespoons fresh coriander, chopped

2 eggs, lightly beaten

Method

1. Mince the fish fillets with a pinch of salt and lemon juice in a blender or food processor.
2. Heat one tablespoon of oil in a wok; add the ginger, garlic, onion and celery and sauté for one minute. Add the

minced fish and red chilli paste and sauté for two to three minutes. Stir in the vinegar; take the wok off the heat and set aside to cool.

3. When the fish mixture is completely cold, add the cornflour, white pepper powder and fresh coriander and mix well.
4. Add the lightly beaten eggs and salt and knead the mixture into a dough. Divide the fish mixture into twenty equal portions.
5. Grease the palms of your hands; roll and slightly flatten each portion of the fish mixture on your palm into a round patty.
6. Heat a non-stick frying pan. Arrange as many fish cakes as will fit in a single layer and drizzle a little oil around. When one side turns golden brown flip over, drizzle a little more oil and fry till the other side turns golden brown. Drain on absorbent paper. Serve hot.

SPINACH-STUFFED CHILLIES

Ingredients

½ bunch (125 grams) spinach, blanched and chopped

12-16 large green chillies, slit and seeded

1 medium onion, finely chopped

½ cup fresh mushrooms, chopped

50 grams processed cheese, grated

1 teaspoon oil

½ teaspoon cumin powder

½ teaspoon red chilli powder

Salt to taste

¼ cup breadcrumbs

Oil for greasing

Method

1. Heat the oil in a pan; add the chopped onions and cook, stirring continuously, till the onions turn light golden brown. Add the chopped mushrooms and cook for another two to three minutes.
2. Add the spinach and cook for two minutes more. Add the cumin powder, chilli powder and salt. Mix well.
3. Set aside to cool. Add the breadcrumbs and grated cheese to the mixture.
4. Stuff the green chillies with the spinach and mushroom mixture and bake in a preheated oven at 200ºC/400ºF/Gas Mark 6 for about 20 minutes or until the chillies soften. Serve hot.

KEEMA BHARI MIRCH

INGREDIENTS

500 grams minced mutton

8-12 large Bhavnagri green chillies

¼ cup oil

1 teaspoon caraway seeds

2 medium onions, chopped

2 tablespoons ginger-garlic paste

Salt to taste

½ teaspoon turmeric powder

2 teaspoons red chilli powder

2 tablespoons chopped fresh coriander

1 medium onion, sliced

½ cup yogurt, whisked

1 tablespoon lemon juice

Garam Masala
4 cloves

2 green cardamoms

1 inch cinnamon

½ teaspoon caraway seeds

METHOD

1. Slit the green chillies and remove the stems and seeds. Grind together all the ingredients for the *garam masala*.

2. Heat two tablespoons of oil in a pan; add half the caraway seeds and half the chopped onions and sauté for one minute. Add half the ginger-garlic paste, stir and add the minced mutton and sauté for five minutes. Add salt to taste, a pinch of turmeric powder and half the chilli powder. Mix well and cook over high heat till completely dry. Set aside to cool.
3. Mix half the fresh coriander into the cooled mince.
4. Stuff the chillies with half the mince and if need be, secure with toothpicks.
5. In a separate pan, heat the remaining oil and add the remaining caraway seeds. Add the rest of the chopped onions along with the sliced onion. Fry till golden brown; add the remaining ginger-garlic paste, turmeric powder and chilli powder. Mix well and add the remaining mince.
6. Add the yogurt and cook for two to three minutes. Stir in half a cup of water. Place the stuffed chillies in the *masala*. Sprinkle with some salt, the *garam masala* powder, remaining fresh coriander and lemon juice. Cover and cook over low heat for ten to fifteen minutes. Serve hot.

ANDHRA CHILLI CHICKEN

Ingredients

1 medium chicken

Salt to taste

4 tablespoons lemon juice

2 inches ginger

6-8 garlic cloves

8-10 curry leaves

8-10 whole red chillies

2 tablespoons rice

½ cup yogurt

¼ cup groundnut oil

¼ refined flour

½ cup fresh coriander, finely chopped

Method

1. Clean, wash and cut the chicken into four pieces (two legs and two breasts). Make four to five, half-inch deep slits on the chicken pieces. Apply the salt and two tablespoons lemon juice and keep aside.
2. Grind together the ginger, garlic, curry leaves, whole red chillies and rice to a smooth paste along with the remaining lemon juice. Stir in the yogurt and whisk well to attain a smooth consistency. Add salt to taste.
3. Apply the yogurt mixture liberally on the chicken pieces and leave to marinate for four to six hours, preferably in the refrigerator.

4. Heat the oil in a pan, roll the marinated chicken in the refined flour; shake off the excess flour and shallow-fry. Cook for one minute, turn over the chicken pieces and cook for another minute.
5. Lower the heat and cook for five to six minutes, turning the chicken pieces frequently so that the chicken cooks and browns evenly on all sides. Remove and drain on absorbent paper.
6. Transfer the chicken to a shallow pan and keep on medium heat. Sprinkle the chopped coriander, two tablespoons water and cover with a fitting lid. Lower the heat and cook for five minutes or until the chicken is completely cooked.
7. Serve hot.

CHILLI-CHEESE TOAST

Ingredients

4-6 green chillies, finely chopped

1½ cups cheese, grated

8 bread slices

½ cup fresh coriander, chopped

1 medium onion, chopped

1 medium capsicum (optional), seeded and chopped

1 teaspoon black peppercorns, crushed

Salt to taste

Method

1. In a bowl, mix the green chillies, cheese, fresh coriander, onion, capsicum, crushed peppercorns and salt. Divide the mixture into eight equal portions.
2. Toast the bread slices on one side on a *tawa*.
3. Spread the cheese mixture on the non-toasted side of bread slices.
4. Grill in an oven preheated at 180ºC/350ºF/Gas Mark 4 until the cheese melts and turns golden brown.
5. Cut each slice diagonally into two and serve hot with a sauce of your choice.

PRAWN VARUVAL

Ingredients

12-16 (150 grams) medium prawns, peeled and deveined

1 inch ginger, peeled

6-8 garlic cloves, peeled

1 teaspoon cumin powder

1 tablespoon Tamarind Pulp (Page 90)

2 tablespoons red chilli powder

½ teaspoon turmeric powder

Salt to taste

2 tablespoons rice flour

¼ cup oil

1 tablespoon lemon juice

Method

1. Grind together the ginger and garlic to a fine paste. Mix the ginger-garlic paste with cumin powder, tamarind pulp, chilli powder, turmeric powder, salt, rice flour and two tablespoons of oil.
2. Marinate the prawns in the mixture for at least two hours in a refrigerator.
3. Heat the remaining oil in a pan, add the marinated prawns and cook for a minute on high heat. Turn over the prawns and cook for another minute.
4. Lower heat and cook for two to three minutes, turning the prawns occasionally to cook evenly. Drain on absorbent paper, sprinkle with the lemon juice and serve hot.

MIRCHI BHAJIYA

Ingredients

8 large chillies, slit and seeded

1 cup gram flour

1 teaspoon baking powder

½ teaspoon asafoetida

1 teaspoon red chilli powder

Salt to taste

1 tablespoon oil + for deep-frying

½ teaspoon mustard seeds

4-5 garlic cloves, crushed

¼ teaspoon turmeric powder

2 large potatoes, boiled and mashed

Method

1. Whisk the gram flour, baking powder, asafoetida, chilli powder and salt with approximately one cup of water in a deep bowl to make a smooth batter. Set aside for about ten minutes.
2. To make the filling, heat one tablespoon of oil in a pan and add the mustard seeds. When they begin to splutter add the crushed garlic and sauté on medium heat till fragrant. Add the turmeric powder and the mashed potatoes and mix well. Add the salt and mix. Remove from heat and set aside to cool.

3. Divide the mixture into eight equal portions and stuff each chilli with a portion of the filling.
4. Heat sufficient oil in a *kadai*. Dip the chillies in the gram flour batter and deep-fry till golden and crisp. Drain on absorbent paper. Serve hot.

STUFFED CHILLIES

INGREDIENTS

8 large Bhavnagri green chillies, slit and seeded

Salt to taste

5 tablespoons oil

A pinch of asafoetida

½ teaspoon mustard seeds

1 teaspoon turmeric powder

2 cups grated fresh coconut

1 teaspoon red chilli powder

½ teaspoon fennel powder

¼ teaspoon cumin powder

¼ teaspoon coriander powder

1 small unripe green mango, peeled and grated

A few sprigs of fresh coriander, finely chopped

METHOD

1. Apply a little salt and set aside for thirty minutes. Wash and drain well.
2. Heat two tablespoons of oil and sauté asafoetida, mustard seeds and turmeric powder.

3. Add the coconut and sauté till lightly coloured.
4. Add the chilli powder, fennel powder, cumin powder, coriander powder and grated mango. Sauté till well mixed and dry.
5. Add the salt and chopped coriander and remove from heat.
6. Stuff the mixture into the chillies.
7. Heat the remaining oil in a shallow pan. Add the stuffed chillies, cover and cook for five minutes.
8. Serve hot.

MIRCHI KA SALAN

Ingredients

18-20 large green chillies

2 tablespoons oil + for deep-frying

2 tablespoons sesame seeds

1 tablespoon coriander seeds

1 teaspoon cumin seeds

½ cup roasted peanuts

2 dried red chillies

1 inch ginger, roughly chopped

6-8 garlic cloves, roughly chopped

1 teaspoon mustard seeds

8-10 curry leaves

1 medium onion, grated

1 teaspoon turmeric powder

2 tablespoons Tamarind Pulp (page 90)

Salt to taste

Method

1. Wash, wipe and slit green chillies lengthways without cutting them into two. Deep-fry in hot oil for one minute. Drain on absorbent paper and set aside.

2. Dry-roast sesame seeds, coriander seeds and cumin seeds. Grind together the roasted seeds, peanuts, red chillies, ginger and garlic to a paste.
3. Heat two tablespoons of oil in a pan; add mustard seeds. When they begin to splutter, add the curry leaves and grated onion and sauté till light golden brown.
4. Add the turmeric powder and mix well. Add the *masala* paste and cook for three minutes, stirring continuously. Stir in one and a half cups of water and bring to a boil. Lower the heat and simmer for ten minutes.
5. Add the tamarind pulp, dissolved in half a cup of water if it is too thick.
6. Add fried green chillies and salt and cook on low heat for eight to ten minutes.

Chef's Tip

In Hyderabad, Mirchi ka Salan is traditionally served as an accompaniment to biryanis. Some people like to add grated coconut to the *masala* paste, but I prefer it without. This gravy is referred to as "tili aur falli" gravy (til=sesame seeds, moongphali= peanuts).

CHILLI-GARLIC OKRA

INGREDIENTS

500 grams okra/ladies' fingers

4 tablespoons cornflour

2 tablespoons oil + for deep-frying

6-8 garlic cloves, peeled and chopped

1 medium onion, peeled and sliced

3-4 green chillies, sliced diagonally

1 medium capsicum, seeded and cut into strips

1 tablespoon soy sauce

½ teaspoon MSG (optional)

½ teaspoon white pepper powder

Salt to taste

2 tablespoons red chilli flakes

METHOD

1. Wash, pat dry and trim the tips and tops of the ladies' fingers.
2. Sprinkle two tablespoons of cornflour on ladies' fingers and mix well. Mix the remaining cornflour with one cup of water.
3. Heat the oil in a wok and deep-fry the ladies' fingers until golden brown and

crisp. Remove and drain on absorbent paper.

4. Heat two tablespoons of oil in a wok, add the chopped garlic and stir-fry for a few seconds. Add the sliced onion, green chillies and capsicum and sauté for two to three minutes or until the onion turns translucent.
5. Add the soy sauce, MSG, white pepper powder, salt and cornflour mixture. Cook, stirring continuously, for a couple of minutes, or until the sauce thickens.
6. Add the fried ladies' fingers and toss well to mix. Sprinkle the red chilli flakes and serve hot.

CHILLI-GARLIC NOODLES

INGREDIENTS

3 fresh red chillies, thinly sliced

12-15 garlic cloves, sliced

200 grams eggless noodles

Salt to taste

1 tablespoon oil

3 tablespoons Chilli Oil (page 94)

1 medium onion, sliced

3 spring onion green stalks, finely chopped

1 teaspoon red chilli sauce

¼ teaspoon MSG (optional)

1 teaspoon white vinegar

1 cup bean sprouts

METHOD

1. Boil the noodles in six to eight cups of salted water to which one tablespoon of oil has been added; cook till almost done. Drain, refresh in cold water. Drain again and spread on a large plate to cool.

2 Heat two tablespoons of chilli oil in a wok; add the onion, garlic and red chillies reserving a few slices for garnishing, and stir-fry for two minutes.

3 Add the noodles, spring onion greens, red chilli sauce, MSG, vinegar and salt and cook for two minutes, stirring and

tossing continuously, until noodles are heated through.

4 Add the bean sprouts and the remaining chilli oil and toss to mix.

5 Serve, garnished with the reserved red chillies.

FRIED CHILLI CHICKEN

Ingredients

6-8 green chillies, sliced

2 tablespoons chilli sauce

400 grams boneless chicken, cut into fingers

2 eggs

6 tablespoons cornflour

Salt to taste

2 tablespoons soy sauce

2 medium onions, cut into think slices

8-10 garlic cloves, finely chopped

2 medium green capsicums, cut into thick strips

3 tablespoons oil + for deep-frying

¼ teaspoon MSG (optional)

½ teaspoon peppercorns, crushed

3 cups Chicken Stock (page 79)

2 tablespoons vinegar

Method

1. Mix the eggs, four tablespoons cornflour, salt to taste, one tablespoon each of soy sauce and chilli sauce into the chicken. Marinate for half an hour.
2. Mix the remaining cornflour in half a cup of water and set aside.

3. Heat sufficient oil in a wok and deep-fry the marinated chicken for two minutes. Drain on absorbent paper.

5 Heat three tablespoons of oil in a wok or a pan, add the chopped garlic and stir-fry briefly. Add the onion and sliced green chillies. Continue to stir-fry for a couple of minutes.

6 Add the remaining soy sauce and chilli sauce, MSG, crushed peppercorns, salt to taste and stir in the chicken stock. Bring to a boil and stir in the cornflour mixture.

7 Cook on high heat for a minute or until the sauce starts to thicken. Add the fried chicken, capsicums, vinegar and cook for a minute on high heat, stirring continuously and serve hot.

CHICKEN CHETTINAD

INGREDIENTS

1 whole chicken (1 kilogram), cut into 12 pieces

6–8 dried red chillies

½ fresh coconut, grated

2 teaspoons poppy seeds

1 teaspoon coriander seeds

½ teaspoon cumin seeds

3 green cardamoms

2 cloves

1 inch cinnamon

½ star anise

1 teaspoon fennel seeds

2 teaspoons ginger, chopped

2 teaspoons garlic, chopped

½ cup oil

1 large onion, chopped

10–12 curry leaves

3 medium tomatoes, chopped

1 teaspoon red chilli powder

½ teaspoon turmeric powder

1 tablespoon lemon juice

Salt to taste

A few sprigs of fresh coriander

Method

1. Sauté the red chillies, grated coconut, poppy seeds, coriander seeds, cumin seeds, cardamoms, cloves, cinnamon, star anise and fennel seeds separately in a little oil; grind together the sautéed spices with the ginger and garlic to a paste.
2. Heat the oil in a *degchi* and fry onions till golden. Add the curry leaves and the ground paste and sauté for a few minutes. Add the tomatoes, chilli powder and turmeric powder.
3. Add the chicken and mix well. Cook for five minutes, add two cups of water and the lemon juice; cover and cook till the chicken is done.
4. Garnish with fresh coriander and serve hot with boiled rice or *paranthas*.

Chef's Tip

Try this dish without the coconut for a different flavour.

MIRCHI MURGH

Ingredients

4 chicken legs
A few sprigs of fresh coriander, chopped
4 teaspoons oil
4 tablespoons tomato purée
¼ teaspoon sugar
Salt to taste

Marinade

5-6 green chillies, roughly chopped
1 medium onion, roughly chopped
2 inches ginger, roughly chopped
4 garlic cloves, roughly chopped
Salt to taste
2 teaspoons lemon juice

Paste

4-5 whole red chillies
2 tablespoons coriander seeds
1 teaspoon cumin seeds
1 inch cinnamon
4 cloves
4 green cardamoms

Method

1. Clean, deskin, wash and cut each leg into two at the knee joint.
2. For the marinade, grind together the onion, ginger, garlic and green chillies until smooth. Stir in the salt and lemon juice.
3. Rub the marinade into the chicken. Cover and leave to marinate for four to six hours in the refrigerator. Remove from refrigerator at least thirty minutes before cooking.
4. Grind together all the ingredients for the paste till smooth using little water.
5. Place the marinated chicken in a microwave-safe bowl. Cook, covered, on HIGH (100%) for eight minutes, stirring once. Mix in the paste and cook, covered, on HIGH (100%) for three minutes, stirring once. Stir in the oil, tomato purée, sugar and salt to taste. Cover and cook on MEDIUM (70%) for ten minutes.
6. Garnish with fresh coriander and serve hot.

CHILLI-GARLIC CRAB

Ingredients

3-4 dried red chillies, broken into two
2 tablespoons red chilli paste
14-16 garlic cloves, peeled and crushed
2 large crabs
2 tablespoons cornflour
4 tablespoons oil
1 tablespoon soy sauce
1 teaspoon sugar
¼ teaspoon MSG (optional)
1½ cups Fish or Chicken Stock (page 79)
½ teaspoon black peppercorns, crushed
Salt to taste
2 tablespoons dry sherry (optional)
1 tablespoon vinegar
2 tablespoons sesame oil
2 spring onion greens, chopped

Method

1. Separate the claws and cut each crab into four pieces. Wash and remove the gills and stomach sac. Crack the claws lightly, wash thoroughly and drain well.
2. Mix the cornflour with half a cup of water.

3. Heat the oil in a wok or a pan; add crushed garlic and red chillies and stir-fry for a few seconds. Add the red chilli paste, soy sauce, sugar, MSG and the crab. Continue to stir-fry for two or three minutes.
4. Stir in the stock and cook for two minutes, or until the crabs are cooked.
5. Stir in the cornflour mixture and cook for one minute, or until the sauce starts to thicken. Add the crushed peppercorns, salt, dry sherry and vinegar.
6. Drizzle sesame oil over and serve hot, garnished with chopped spring onion greens.

Chef's Tip

Buy fresh crabs and have them cut by your fishmonger, as it can be very messy to cut crabs in your kitchen.

BUNDLES OF VEGETABLES IN CHILLI-HONEY-SESAME SAUCE

Ingredients

5-6 oyster mushrooms

1 medium carrot, cut into thin strips

1 medium zucchini, cut into thin strips

2 slices bamboo shoot, cut into thin strips

1 medium red capsicum, cut into thin strips

1 medium yellow capsicum, cut into thin strips

1 medium green capsicum, cut into thin strips

1 tablespoon sesame seeds, toasted

3 cups Vegetable Stock (page 12)

1 inch fresh ginger, peeled and finely chopped

Salt to taste

2 spring onion greens, cut into thin strips

Sauce

1 teaspoon red chilli sauce

1 tablespoon honey

2 tablespoons sesame oil

5-6 garlic cloves, peeled and finely chopped

1¼ cup Vegetable Stock (page 12)

¼ teaspoon MSG (optional)

Salt to taste

1 tablespoon wine

5-6 black peppercorns

1 teaspoon vinegar

1 teaspoon soya sauce

1 tablespoon cornflour

Method

1. Soak the dried mushrooms in warm water for twenty to thirty minutes. Drain and slice the mushrooms.
2. Bring the vegetable stock to a boil; add chopped ginger and salt. Blanch the vegetables one at a time in boiling stock. Drain and reserve the stock and the vegetables.
3. Make up bundles of assorted vegetables; tie each bundle around the middle with a spring onion stalk. Keep warm.
4. To make the sauce, heat oil in a pan, add garlic and sauté for one or two minutes. Add one cup of vegetable stock and the rest of the ingredients for the sauce, except cornflour, and bring to a boil.
5. Mix the cornflour with a quarter cup of vegetable stock and stir into the hot sauce. Simmer for a few minutes.
6. Pour the sauce over the vegetable bundles, coating them evenly. Sprinkle with sesame seeds and serve immediately.

CHICKEN WITH CHILLI JAM

Ingredients

3 (150 grams each) boneless chicken breasts, cut into strips

2 teaspoons oil

4 shallots, chopped

½ head of broccoli, cut into small florets

12 snow peas, halved

¼ cup roasted cashew nuts

2 tablespoons light soy sauce

Salt to taste

White pepper powder to taste

Chilli Jam

4 fresh red chillies, sliced

1/3 cup sugar

2 teaspoons oil

1½ inches ginger, shredded

2 tablespoons lemon juice

Method

1. To make the chilli jam, heat the oil in a wok over medium heat; add the red chillies and ginger and stir-fry for one minute.

2 Add the sugar, lemon juice and one-third cup of water. Cook, stirring continuously, for three minutes, or till thick. Remove from heat and keep warm.

3 For the chicken, heat the oil in a separate wok; add the chicken and shallots and stir-fry for three minutes, or until chicken is lightly browned.

4 Add the broccoli, snow peas, cashew nuts, soy sauce, salt and white pepper powder and stir-fry for three minutes, or until the vegetables change colour.

5 Place the chicken on a serving plate, top with the chilli jam and serve immediately.

Chef's Tip

You can also serve hot and tangy Chilli Jam with grilled fish and prawns.

HONEY-CHILLI CHICKEN

Ingredients

4 tablespoons honey

2 fresh red chillies, slit

1 tablespoon red chilli flakes

400 grams boneless chicken, cut into 1-inch cubes

3 tablespoons oil + for deep-frying

1½ tablespoons cornflour

1 teaspoon light soy sauce

¼ teaspoon MSG (optional)

½ teaspoon white pepper powder

Salt to taste

1½ cups Chicken Stock (page 79)

2-3 garlic cloves, chopped

1 tablespoon toasted sesame seeds

2 spring onion green stalks, chopped

Method

1. Heat the oil in a wok and deep-fry the chicken cubes on high heat for half a minute. Drain on absorbent paper.
2. Mix the cornflour, soy sauce, MSG, white pepper powder and salt to taste with the chicken stock.

3. Heat three tablespoons of oil in a wok or pan; add the garlic and red chilli flakes and stir-fry for a few seconds. Add the fresh red chillies and stir-fry.

4. Stir in the sauce and spice mixture. Cook, stirring continuously, for one minute or until the sauce starts to thicken.

5. Add the fried chicken and honey and cook for one minute more. Sprinkle toasted sesame seeds and serve hot, garnished with spring onion greens.

FRIED CHILLI PRAWNS

Ingredients

16 medium prawns, shelled and deveined

2 tablespoons lemon juice

1 tablespoon chilli sauce

Salt to taste

6 tablespoons cornflour

4 tablespoons oil + for deep-frying

2 inches ginger, finely chopped

6-8 garlic cloves, finely chopped

4-6 green chillies, sliced diagonally

2 spring onions, chopped

2 tablespoons soy sauce

½ teaspoon white pepper powder

¼ teaspoon MSG (optional)

1teaspoon sugar

1 cup fish or Chicken Stock (page 79)

1 medium capsicum

Method

1. Mix one tablespoon of lemon juice, chilli sauce and salt to taste with the prawns.

2 Roll the prawns in four tablespoons of cornflour. Heat sufficient oil in a

wok, add the prawns and deep-fry for a minute. Do not overcook. Drain on absorbent paper.

3 Mix the remaining cornflour in half a cup of water and set aside.

4 Heat four tablespoons of oil in a wok or a pan; add the chopped ginger, garlic, sliced green chillies and stir-fry briefly. Add the chopped spring onions, reserving some greens for garnishing, and continue to stir-fry for a couple of minutes more.

5 Add the soy sauce, white pepper powder, MSG, sugar, salt to taste and immediately stir in the stock. Add the fried prawns, capsicum strips and stir-fry for a couple of minutes.

6 Stir in the cornflour mixture and cook for a minute more or until the sauce coats the prawns. Stir in the remaining lemon juice and serve hot, garnished with chopped spring onion greens.

CHEF'S TIP

If you are using large prawns, leave the tips of the tails on for better presentation.

GREEN CHILLI CHICKEN

INGREDIENTS

1 cup small green chillies

3 green chillies, chopped

1 whole (800 grams) chicken, cut into 1½-inch pieces

2 medium onions, quartered

10 garlic cloves

1½ inches ginger, sliced

½ cup chopped fresh coriander

Salt to taste

3 tablespoons oil

¾ teaspoon cumin seeds

¼ teaspoon turmeric powder

1 teaspoon roasted cumin powder

2 teaspoons coriander powder

1 teaspoon *garam masala* powder

METHOD

1. Grind together the chopped green chillies, onions, garlic, ginger, fresh coriander and salt. Marinate the chicken in this mixture for about half an hour.

2. Heat the oil in a wok or *kadai* and add the cumin seeds. When they begin to change colour add the turmeric powder. Add the marinated chicken and small green chillies and mix well. Add the cumin powder and coriander powder and stir to mix.
3. Add the *garam masala* powder and adjust the seasoning. Stir in half a cup of water, cover and cook over medium heat for eight to ten minutes.
4. Lower the heat and cook for another eight to ten minutes or till the chicken is cooked. Serve hot.

JUMBO PRAWNS IN HONEY-CHILLI SAUCE

INGREDIENTS

8 jumbo prawns

2 tablespoons honey

2 teaspoons red chilli sauce

1 teaspoon red chilli flakes

2 tablespoons cornflour

½ teaspoon black peppercorns, crushed

Salt to taste

1 tablespoon + 1 teaspoon soy sauce

1 teaspoon ginger paste

2 tablespoons oil + for deep-frying

10-12 garlic cloves, crushed

1 medium onion, chopped

¾ cup tomato ketchup

1 teaspoon ginger paste

¼ teaspoon crushed black peppercorns

1 tablespoon lemon juice

3-4 spring onion greens, roughly chopped

METHOD

1. Peel and devein the prawns, keeping the tails intact; wash thoroughly under running water.
2. Place the prawns in a bowl with the cornflour, crushed peppercorns, salt,

one tablespoon soy sauce and ginger paste. Mix well and leave to marinate for fifteen minutes.

3. Heat the oil in a deep pan and deep-fry the prawns for half a minute. Drain on absorbent paper.
4. Heat two tablespoons of oil in another pan; add crushed garlic and sauté on high heat till slightly burnt. Add the onion and sauté till soft.
5. Add the tomato ketchup, one teaspoon soy sauce, red chilli sauce, ginger paste, crushed peppercorns and red chilli flakes, and stir-fry for two minutes. Add fried prawns and stir.
6. Add the honey, salt and lemon juice and cook for one minute. Add the spring onion greens; mix and cook for one minute more. Serve hot.

GOAN CHILLI CHICKEN

Ingredients

6 green chillies, chopped
2 whole red chillies
8 chicken thighs
1 small onion, roughly chopped
2 inches ginger, roughly chopped
4 garlic cloves, roughly chopped
Salt to taste
4 teaspoons lemon juice
1 teaspoon cumin seeds
2 tablespoons coriander seeds
4 green cardamoms
4 cloves
1 inch cinnamon stick
4 tablespoons ghee
4 tablespoons tomato purée
¼ teaspoon sugar
A few sprigs of fresh coriander, chopped
1 tablespoon vinegar

Method

1. Clean the chicken thighs and remove the skin. Wash and drain thoroughly. Grind together the onion, ginger, garlic

and half of the chopped green chillies to a paste.

2. Add the salt and lemon juice to the paste; marinate the chicken in it for two hours, preferably in a refrigerator.
3. Dry-roast the cumin seeds, coriander seeds, whole red chillies, green cardamoms, cloves and cinnamon; grind to a powder.
4. Heat two tablespoons of ghee in a pan. Add the marinated chicken and cook on high heat.
5. When the chicken is half done, add the *masala* powder and mix well.
6. Add the remaining ghee and tomato purée and let cook further.
7. Add the sugar and adjust salt and cook till the chicken is done.
8. Add the remaining chopped green chillies and chopped fresh coriander.
9. Remove from the heat. Add the vinegar, stir and serve immediately.

BRAISED SICHUAN CHICKEN

Ingredients

500 gms boneless chicken breasts, cut into 1-inch cubes

6-8 black mushrooms

1 ½ tablespoons cornflour

2 teaspoons hot soy bean paste

1 teaspoon sugar

½ teaspoon white pepper powder

1 tablespoon rice wine (optional)

Salt to taste

¼ teaspoon MSG (optional)

1 cup Chicken Stock (*see below*)

2 tablespoons oil

1 inch ginger, thickly sliced

4-5 whole red chillies, broken into half

2 spring onions, cut into 1-inch pieces

2 tablespoons Chilli Oil (page 94)

Method

1. Soak black mushrooms in sufficient hot water for fifteen minutes. Drain and cut them into quarters.
2. Mix the cornflour in half a cup of water. Mix the hot soy bean paste, sugar, white pepper powder, rice wine,

salt to taste and MSG with the chicken stock.

3. Heat two tablespoons of oil in a wok or pan. Add the sliced ginger, red chillies and stir-fry briefly. Add the chicken, spring onions, mushrooms and continue to stir-fry for a couple of minutes more.

4. Stir in the sauce and spice mix, cook on medium heat for a minute and stir in the cornflour mixture.

5. Cook on high heat for half a minute or until the sauce coats the chicken well, stirring and tossing continuously. Drizzle the chilli oil and serve hot.

Chicken Stock

Boil 200 grams chicken bones in water for 5 minutes. Drain and discard water. Boil blanched bones with a roughly chopped carrot, celery stalk, leek, 2-3 parsley stalks, 6-7 black peppercorns, 5-6 cloves, 1 bay leaf and 10 cups of water. Remove any scum which rises to the surface and replace it with more cold water. Simmer for at least one hour. Remove from heat, strain, cool and store in a refrigerator till further use.

MIRCH KORMA

INGREDIENTS

800 grams mutton on the bone, cut into 1½-inch pieces

15 Kashmiri red chillies

4 tablespoons oil

½ teaspoon cumin seeds

3 green cardamoms

3 cloves

1 cup yogurt

2 teaspoons fennel powder

½ teaspoon cinnamon powder

1 teaspoon dried ginger powder

Salt to taste

METHOD

1. Soak the Kashmiri chillies in one cup of hot water for five minutes. Drain, remove the seeds and grind with one cup of water to a fine paste.
2. Heat the oil in a thick-bottomed pan. Add the cumin seeds, cardamoms and cloves and sauté for one minute. Add the yogurt and sauté till light brown.
3. Add the mutton and sauté for four to five minutes.
4. Add the fennel powder, cinnamon powder, ginger powder and salt and continue to sauté for a few minutes.

5. Pass the chilli paste through a piece of muslin and add to the mutton gradually, stirring continuously. Add one and a half cups of water and bring the mixture to a boil. Lower heat and simmer till the oil separates and the mutton is tender. Serve hot.

DEEP-FRIED CHILLI FISH

INGREDIENTS

1 whole (1 kilogram) fish such as Pomfret, cleaned

4 fresh red chillies, chopped

4 coriander roots

3 garlic cloves, crushed

6-7 black peppercorns, crushed

Salt to taste

Oil for deep-frying

Red Chilli Sauce

$^{2}/_{3}$ cup sugar

8 fresh red chillies, sliced

4 medium onions, sliced

$^{1}/_{3}$ cup vinegar

Salt to taste

2 tablespoons Chilli Oil (page 94)

METHOD

1. Make diagonal slits on both sides of the fish.

2 Grind together the fresh red chillies, coriander roots, garlic, peppercorns and salt to a paste.

3 Spread the paste on both sides of the fish and marinate for thirty minutes.

4 To make the red chilli sauce, place the sugar, red chillies, onions, vinegar, salt and one-third cup of water in a pan; cook over low heat, stirring continuously, till the sugar dissolves completely and the sauce thickens. Keep warm.

5 Heat the oil in a large wok. Deep-fry the fish till crisp on both sides. Drain on absorbent paper.

6 Serve hot with the red chilli sauce.

CHEF'S TIP

Coriander roots are widely used in Thai cooking. Scrape off the outer layer of thick roots before using.

MIRCHICHA THECHA

INGREDIENTS

8-9 green chillies, roughly chopped

1 tablespoon oil

¼ cup white sesame seeds

7-8 garlic cloves, roughly chopped

½ cup grated coconut,

1 tablespoon fresh coriander, roughly chopped

Salt to taste

METHOD

1. Heat the oil on a *tawa*, add the green chillies, sesame seeds, garlic, coconut and fresh coriander. Sauté for three to four minutes. Remove from heat and set aside to cool. Add the salt and mix.
2. Grind coarsely in a blender or pound in a mortar with a pestle.
3. Transfer to a bowl and serve as an accompaniment.

SWEET CHILLI CHUTNEY

Ingredients

18-20 Kashmiri chillies, broken into bits

3 medium tomatoes, chopped

Salt to taste

8-10 garlic cloves, peeled and chopped

2 tablespoons oil

2 tablespoons sugar

2 tablespoons honey

Method

1. Process the red chillies, tomatoes, half a cup of water, salt and garlic in a blender, to a smooth paste.
2. Heat the oil in a pan, add the paste and cook for a few minutes. Add the sugar and bring to a boil. Cook for ten minutes. Remove the scum if any.
3. Stir in the honey and remove the pan off the heat.
4. Cool and store.

PEPPER-CHILLI SAUCE

INGREDIENTS

3 medium green capsicums, cut into ¼-inch cubes

7-8 black peppercorns, freshly crushed

1 teaspoon red chilli powder

6 medium tomatoes, chopped

1 medium onion, chopped

4-5 cloves

1 inch cinnamon stick

½ cup brown sugar

¼ cup cider vinegar

1 bay leaf

Salt to taste

METHOD

1. Place the cloves and cinnamon in a microwave-safe plate and dry-roast on HIGH (100%) for two minutes. Grind to a coarse powder.
2. Place the tomatoes, onion, brown sugar, cider vinegar (replace with any available vinegar), clove-cinnamon powder, chilli powder and bay leaf in a large microwave-safe bowl.
3. Cover and cook on HIGH (100%) for fifteen minutes. Remove.
4. Stir in the capsicums, salt and add freshly crushed peppercorns.

5. Cook, uncovered, on HIGH (100%) for fifteen minutes or until the mixture thickens.
6. Remove the bay leaf and pour into hot, sterilised jars.
7. Seal and cover. Best stored in the refrigerator.

GOAN CHILLI PICKLE

INGREDIENTS

500 grams mild green chillies,

8-10 dried red Reshampatti chillies

1 cup vinegar

200 grams garlic, peeled and chopped

200 grams fresh ginger, peeled and chopped

½ cup Tamarind Pulp (*see below*)

1 cup sesame oil

¾ cup sugar

½ cup salt

1 teaspoon split fenugreek seeds, powdered

METHOD

1. Crush the green chillies with a little salt in a blender. Soak the red chillies in vinegar.
2. Crush the garlic and ginger. Grind the red chillies with vinegar and tamarind pulp.
3. Heat the oil in a pan to smoking point. Cool slightly and add the crushed garlic, ginger and green chillies and sauté on high heat for four to five minutes.
4. Add the red chilli paste and continue to cook, stirring continuously, for another four to five minutes.

5. Add the sugar and salt and stir. Add the powdered fenugreek seeds and mix well. Cook a little longer.

6. Transfer to sterilised bottles and leave to cool. Store in the refrigerator.

Chef's Tip

This chilli pickle tastes wonderful as a spread on fresh bread.

Tamarind Pulp

Soak 75 grams tamarind in 100 ml warm water for ten to fifteen minutes. Grind to a smooth paste and strain to remove any fibres. Store in an airtight container in the refrigerator.

VARHADI THECHA

Ingredients

20-25 dried red chillies

2 tablespoons oil

12-16 garlic cloves, roughly chopped

1 inch ginger, roughly chopped

1 tablespoon lemon juice

4 tablespoons vinegar

Salt to taste

½ teaspoon sugar

Method

1. Heat the oil in a pan, add the garlic and ginger.
2. Stir-fry briefly, add the red chillies and continue stir-frying for half a minute more. Remove from heat and cool. Grind with the lemon juice, vinegar, salt and sugar into a fine paste.
3. Serve as an accompaniment.

RED CHILLI-GARLIC CHUTNEY

Ingredients

10 dried red chillies, seeded

12 large garlic cloves, peeled and chopped

2 teaspoons lemon juice

Sea salt to taste

1 teaspoon cumin powder

Method

1. Soak the red chillies in one and a half cups of water for half an hour. Drain.
2. Grind the red chillies and garlic cloves with lemon juice to a fine paste. Add a little water if necessary.
3. Add sea salt and cumin powder and mix well.
4. Serve as an accompaniment.

SWEET CHILLI SAUCE

Ingredients

18-20 Kashmiri chillies, seeded

2 medium tomatoes, chopped

3-4 garlic cloves, chopped

2 tablespoons sugar

1 tablespoon oil

1 tablespoon soy sauce

Salt to taste

Method

1. Grind together the red chillies, tomatoes and garlic into a smooth paste.
2. Combine the sugar and oil in a microwave-safe bowl and cook, uncovered, on HIGH (100%) for two minutes. Remove.
3. Add the paste, soy sauce, salt to taste and one cup of water. Mix well. Cook, uncovered, on MEDIUM (70%) for two minutes. Remove and stir once. Cook, uncovered, further for two minutes. Remove and serve when cool.

CHILLI OIL

Ingredients

250 ml groundnut oil

6 tablespoons dried red chillies, chopped

2-3 teaspoons red chilli powder

1-2 tablespoons sesame oil

Method

1. Heat the oil in a wok. Add the red chillies and cook on low heat for at least ten minutes. Set aside to cool.
2. When cool add the chilli powder and sesame oil. Cover and let it stand for at least twelve hours. Strain into a sterilised bottle and store in a cool, dark place.

CHILLI-GARLIC SAUCE

Ingredients

20 whole red chillies

8 garlic cloves

8 tablespoons vinegar

1 tablespoon sugar

Salt to taste

1½ tablespoons sesame oil

Method

1. Mix all the ingredients except oil and blend to a fine paste in a processor.
2. Add the oil and blend well. Keep refrigerated.

GLOSSARY

ENGLISH	HINDI
Apple	saeb
Asafoetida	hing
Baby potatoes	chhote aloo
Basil, fresh	tulsi ki pattiyan
Bay leaves	tez patta
Bean sprouts	ankurit moong
Breadcrumbs	bread ka choora
Capsicum, green	hari Shimla mirch
Capsicum, red	lal shimla mirch
Capsicum, yellow	pili Shimla mirch
Caraway	shahi jeera
Cardamoms, black	badi elaichi
Cardamoms, green	chhoti elaichi
Carrot	gajar
Cashew nuts	kaju
Cherry tomatoes	chhote tamatar
Chicken	murgh
Chillies, dried red	sookhi lal mirch

ENGLISH	HINDI
Chillies, fresh red	taazi lal mirch
Chillies, green	hari mirch
Cinnamon	dalchini
Cloves	laung
Coconut	nariyal
Coriander seeds	dhania
Coriander, fresh	hara dhania
Cottage cheese	paneer
Crabs	kekde
Cream	malai
Cucumber	kakdi/kheera
Cumin seeds	jeera
Curry leaves	kadhi patta
Egg	anda
Fennel seeds	saunf
Fenugreck leaves, dried	kasuri methi
Fenugreek seeds	methi dana
Garlic cloves	lehsun ki kaliyan

ENGLISH	HINDI
Ginger, dried	sonth
Ginger, fresh	adrak
Gram flour	besan
Honey	shahad/madhu
Ladies' fingers	bhindi
Lemon	nimbu
Lettuce	salad patta
Mint leaves, fresh	pudina ke pattiyan
Mushroom	dhingri/khumb/ guchhi/kukurmutta
Mustard seeds	rai
Olives	jaitun
Orange	narangi/santara
Papaya	papita
Peanuts	moongphali
Pear	nashpati
Peppercorns, black	kali mirch
Peppercorns, white	safed mirch
Pineapple	ananas
Pomegranate	anar
Poppy seeds	khuskhus

ENGLISH	HINDI
Prawns	jheenga
Refined flour	maida
Salt, black	kala namak
Sesame seeds	til
Shallots	chhote pyaaz
Spinach leaves	palak ke taze patte
Spring onion	hara pyaaz
Spring onion greens	hare pyaaz ki pattiyan
Star anise	chakri phool/badiyan
Sweetcorn kernels	makai ke dane
Tamarind	imli
Tomato purée	pise hue tamatar
Tomatoes	tamatar
Turmeric powder	haldi
Vermicelli	seviyan
Vinegar	sirka
Yogurt	dahi